Living CHEAPLY in the PHILIPPINES 101 tips to save money

Arthur Crandon LL.B. (Hons.) M.A.

Living CHEAPLY in the PHILIPPINES
101 tips to save money

Copyright Arthur Crandon 2024

All rights reserved. No part of this book may be reproduced, stored in a retrieval system, or transmitted in any form or by any means—electronic, mechanical, photocopying, recording, or otherwise—without the prior written permission of the publisher, except for brief quotations in critical reviews or articles.

This is a work of fiction. Names, characters, places, and incidents are either the product of the author's imagination or used fictitiously. Any resemblance to actual persons, living or dead, events, or locales is entirely coincidental.

ISBN: 9798341461598
Cover design by Lynnie Ceniza
Interior design and formatting by Lynnie Ceniza
Published by Arthur Crandon Publishing
Visit our website: Arthurcrandon.co.uk

DISCLAIMER
The information provided in this book is for general informational purposes only. It does not constitute legal, financial, or professional advice. While every effort has been made to ensure accuracy, the author and publisher assume no responsibility for errors or omissions. Readers should consult with appropriate professionals for specific advice tailored to their individual circumstances.

First Edition: August 2024

Living within a budget – especially in retirement can be a challenge
in the Philippines – especially at a time when prices are rising fast
and pensions are not keeping pace.
This book will help you to stay on track.

CONTENTS

	Acknowledgments	i
1	Essentials	1
2	Money Savings	5
3	Self-Sufficiency	9
4	Financial Stability	13
5	Invest wisely	19
6	Travelling	27
7	Health Matters	37
8	Work related issues	41
9	Additional Information	47

Many people – especially expats – are struggling as their income is fixed but their spending cannot be – and it continues to rise.

You can weather the storm of the financial issues with our book,

1 ESSENTIALS

Let's dive deeper into these practical tips for saving money on food and groceries in the Philippines.

1. ****Keep Track of Your Fridge Inventory**:

    - **Why?**: It's easy to forget what's hiding in the back of your fridge. By maintaining a list, you'll avoid buying duplicates and reduce food waste.

    - **How?**: Use a whiteboard, a smartphone app, or a simple paper list. Jot down items as you add them and cross them off as you use them.

2. **Get Creative with Leftovers**:

   o **Why?**: Leftovers can be transformed into delicious meals, saving you time and money.

   o **How?**: Here are some ideas:
      - Turn yesterday's adobo into a filling for empanadas.
      - Combine leftover rice with scrambled eggs and veggies for a quick fried rice.
      - Mix cooked pasta with canned tuna, olives, and olive oil for a simple pasta salad.
      -

3. **Bulk Buying Basics**:

   o **Why?**: Purchasing in bulk often means lower prices per unit.

   o **How?**:
      - Stock up on non-perishables like rice, beans, and canned goods.
      - Buy frozen fruits and vegetables—they're just as nutritious and last longer.
      - Invest in airtight containers

to keep bulk items fresh.

4. **Leave the Kids at Home**:
    - **Why?**: Kids have a magical ability to add extra items to your cart.
    - **How?**: If possible, do your grocery shopping solo. You'll stick to your list and avoid impulse purchases.

5. **Read Labels and Packaging**:

    - **Why?**: Understanding product details helps you make informed choices.
    - **How?**:
        - Check the weight (grams) and compare prices per gram.
        - Look for expiration dates.
        - Consider nutritional value—sometimes cheaper items aren't the healthiest.

6. **Weekly Menu Planning**:

    - **Why?**: Planning ahead reduces last-minute takeout or restaurant visits.

- **How?**:
  - Sit down once a week and plan your meals.
  - Make a shopping list based on your menu.
  - Stick to the list when you shop.

Remember, these small adjustments can add up over time, leaving you with more pesos in your pocket!

2 MONEY SAVINGS

Let's dive deeper into these practical tips for managing your monthly bills more efficiently.

Monthly Bills: Smart Strategies

1. **Unplug Appliances When Not in Use**:

   o **Why?**: Even when turned off, appliances in standby mode consume "phantom" energy. Unplugging them saves electricity.

   o **How?**: Invest in power strips with switches. Turn off the strip when you're not using devices.

2. **Energy-Efficient Bulbs**:

    o **Why?**: Traditional incandescent bulbs waste energy as heat. LED or CFL bulbs are more efficient and last longer.

    o **How?**: Gradually replace old bulbs with energy-saving alternatives.

3. **Negotiate Internet and Cable Bills**:

    o **Why?**: Providers often have promotional rates or loyalty discounts.

    o **How?**: Call your provider, express your loyalty, and ask for better rates. Consider downgrading plans if you don't need all the features.

4. **Opt for Prepaid Mobile Plans**:

    o **Why?**: Postpaid plans can lead to unexpected charges. Prepaid plans give you control.

- **How?**: Switch to a prepaid plan and monitor your usage.

5. **Cancel Unused Subscriptions**:

    - **Why?**: Subscriptions add up—Netflix, gym memberships, magazines, etc.
6.
    - **How?**: Review your subscriptions. If you're not using them regularly, cancel or downgrade.

Useful Skills for Saving Money:

6. **Learn Basic Repair Skills**:

    - **Why?**: Minor repairs can save you from hiring professionals.

    - **How?**: YouTube tutorials and online guides are your friends. Fix leaky faucets, patch small holes, and replace worn-out parts.

7. **Cook at Home**:

    - **Why?**: Eating out is costly and often less healthy.

- **How?**: Plan meals, batch-cook, and explore simple recipes. Cooking can be fun and rewarding!

8. **Learn to Sew**:

    - **Why?**: Mending clothes extends their life.

    - **How?**: Start with basic stitches. Repair buttons, seams, and small tears.

9. **Grow Your Own Herbs and Veggies**:

    - **Why?**: Fresh produce can be expensive.

    - **How?**: Even a small balcony or windowsill can host potted herbs like basil, mint, or parsley. Tomatoes and peppers thrive in containers too.

Remember, these small adjustments can add up over time, leaving you with more pesos in your pocket!

3 SELF-SUFFICIENCY

Let's dive deeper into these useful skills that can help you save more money and become more self-sufficient.

Useful Skills for Saving Money:

1. **Learn Basic Repair Skills**:

    o **Why?**: Minor household repairs can save you from hiring professionals and paying for their services.

    o **How?**:
    - **Fix Leaky Faucets**: A dripping faucet wastes water and money. Learn to replace washers or seals.

- **Patch Small Holes**: Whether it's a hole in the wall or a torn screen, patch it up yourself.

- **Replace Worn-Out Parts**: Fix loose cabinet handles, doorknobs, or hinges without calling a handyman.

2. **Cook at Home**:

    - **Why?**: Eating out is convenient but expensive. Cooking at home saves money and allows you to control ingredients.

    - **How?**:
        - **Plan Meals**: Create a weekly menu. Base it on what's in your pantry and what's on sale.

        - **Batch Cooking**: Prepare larger portions and freeze leftovers for busy days.

        - **Explore Simple Recipes**: You don't need to be a gourmet chef. Master a few basic dishes that you enjoy.

3. **Learn to Sew**:

   - **Why?**: Clothing repairs extend their lifespan, reducing the need for new purchases.

   - **How?**:
     - **Basic Stitches**: Learn how to sew buttons, mend small tears, and fix seams.
     - **Hemming**: Adjust the length of pants or skirts yourself.
     - **Patch Holes**: Turn ripped jeans into trendy distressed denim.

4. **Grow Your Own Herbs and Veggies**:

   - **Why?**: Fresh produce can be expensive, especially if it's imported.
   - **How?**:
     - **Balcony Gardening**: Even a small balcony can host potted herbs like basil, mint, or parsley.
     - **Window Sill Gardens**: Grow microgreens or small veggies indoors.

- **Tomatoes and Peppers**: These thrive in containers with proper sunlight.

Remember, acquiring these skills not only saves money but also empowers you to take charge of your daily life. Happy learning!

4 FINANCIAL STABILITY

Managing debt is crucial for financial stability, and I'm here to provide more details on effective strategies for handling debt in the Philippines. Let's dive into it!

Managing Debt in the Philippines: Key Strategies

1. **Prioritize High-Interest Debt: Pay Off Credit Cards First**

- **Why?**: Credit card interest rates can be exorbitant. Prioritizing credit card debt helps you avoid accumulating more interest.

- **How?**:
    - **Create a Debt Repayment Plan**: List all your debts, including credit cards. Allocate extra payments toward the highest-interest card

while making minimum payments on others.

- **Snowball Method**: Pay off the smallest debt first, then move to the next. This builds momentum and motivation.

2. **Consolidate Loans: Combine Multiple Debts into One with Lower Interest**

- **Why?**: Consolidation simplifies payments and reduces overall interest.

- **How?**:
    - **Personal Loan**: Apply for a personal loan with a lower interest rate than your existing debts. Use it to pay off other loans.
    - **Balance Transfer**: Transfer high-interest credit card balances to a card with a lower rate (if available).

3. **Avoid Payday Loans: Their Interest Rates Are Sky-High**

- **Why?**: Payday loans often come with astronomical interest rates and short repayment terms.

- **How?**:
  - **Explore Alternatives**: Seek help from family or friends, negotiate with creditors, or consider other loan options.
  - **Emergency Fund**: Build an emergency fund to avoid relying on payday loans during financial crises.

Additional Tips:

- **Negotiate with Creditors**: If you're struggling, communicate with your creditors. They may offer temporary relief or revised payment terms.

- **Seek Legal Assistance**: Consult a financial advisor or lawyer if you're overwhelmed by debt. Legal remedies, such as insolvency proceedings, may be available.

Remember, managing debt requires discipline, planning, and seeking professional advice when necessary. You're not alone—many Filipinos face similar challenges, and there are resources available to help you regain control of your finances.

Let's dive deeper into these practical tips for improving your savings in the Philippines. Whether you're just starting or looking to enhance your financial habits, these strategies can make a significant difference.

Tips to Improve Savings:

1. **Automate Your Savings**:

    - **Why?**: Automation ensures consistency. Set up automatic transfers from your main account to a separate savings account.

    - **How?**: Schedule transfers on payday. Treat savings like a non-negotiable bill.

2. **Create a Budget**:

    - **Why?**: A budget gives you control over your money. It's like a roadmap for your finances.

- **How?**:

    - **Track Income and Expenses**: List all sources of income and categorize expenses (rent, groceries, utilities, etc.).

    - **Allocate Funds**: Assign specific amounts to each category. Prioritize essentials first.

    - **Review Regularly**: Adjust as needed based on changes in income or expenses.

3. **Set Savings Goals**:

    - **Why?**: Having a purpose motivates you to save consistently.

    - **How?**:

        - **Emergency Fund**: Aim for 3 to 6 months' worth of living expenses. This fund cushions you during unexpected events.

- **Travel Fund**: If you love exploring, create a separate fund for your dream trips.

- **Investment Goals**: Whether it's stocks, mutual funds, or real estate, set targets for long-term wealth-building.

Remember, small steps lead to big results. Celebrate progress along the way!

5 INVEST WISELY

Let's dive deeper into personal finance essentials, especially tailored for the Philippines. Managing your money wisely is essential for financial stability and achieving your goals. Here are some practical tips and resources to help you navigate the world of personal finance:

1. **Invest Wisely: Learn About Mutual Funds, Stocks, or Real Estate**

- **Mutual Funds:** These are investment vehicles that pool money from various investors to buy a diversified portfolio of stocks, bonds, or other securities. They're managed by professional fund managers. Research different mutual funds available in the Philippines, understand their risk profiles, and consider investing based on your financial goals.

- **Stocks:** Investing in individual stocks allows you to become a partial owner of a company. Learn about stock market basics, company fundamentals, and how to analyze stocks. Consider starting with blue-chip companies or exploring exchange-traded funds (ETFs) for diversification.

- **Real Estate:** Real estate can be a long-term investment. Understand property values, rental yields, and the local real estate market. Consider factors like location, demand, and potential for appreciation.

2. Avoid Impulsive Purchases: Sleep on It Before Buying

- **Why?:** Impulse buying can derail your budget. Taking time to think before making a purchase helps you differentiate between needs and wants.

- **How?:**
  - Create a Cooling-Off Period: When tempted to buy something, wait 24 hours. If you still want it after that time, consider the purchase.
  - Make a Shopping List: Stick to your list when shopping. Avoid spontaneous purchases.

3. **Use Cash:** It's Harder to Overspend Than with Cards

- **Why?:** Cash transactions make spending more tangible. When you physically see money leaving your wallet, you're more conscious of your expenses.

- **How?:**
  - **Envelope System:** Allocate cash for specific categories (groceries, transportation, entertainment) in separate envelopes. Once the envelope is empty, you stop spending in that category.
  - **Limit Card Usage:** Reserve credit or debit cards for emergencies or planned expenses. Leave them at home when unnecessary.

Additional Resources:

1. **Grit PH:** Explore articles on personal finance tailored to Filipinos. Learn about budgeting, saving, investing, and more.

2. **Wise Personal Finance:** Discover tips and tricks for managing your finances efficiently.

3. **MoneySense Philippines**: MoneySense is a premier magazine on personal finance in the Philippines. It covers earning, saving, spending, borrowing, and investing.

4. **Moneymax Blog:** Read about insurance, credit cards, loans, and other financial topics.

Remember, financial literacy is an ongoing journey. Keep learning, adapt to your circumstances, and make informed choices.

Let's explore these shopping tips in more detail, especially considering the context of shopping in the Philippines. Whether you're a seasoned bargain hunter or just starting, these strategies can help you make smarter choices and save money.

Smart Shopping Tips for the Philippines:

1. **Thrift Stores and Ukay-Ukay (Secondhand Shops)**:

   o **Why?**: Thrift stores and ukay-ukay offer pre-loved items at significantly lower prices.

   o **How?**:
      - **Explore Regularly**: Visit local thrift shops or ukay-ukay markets. You'll find unique clothing, accessories, and even household items.

      - **Inspect Items Carefully**: Look for quality pieces—sometimes you'll stumble upon designer brands or vintage treasures.

2. **Use Loyalty Cards**:

   o **Why?**: Loyalty cards or rewards programs allow you to collect points or earn discounts over time.

- **How?**:

    - **Sign Up**: Join loyalty programs at your favorite stores or supermarkets.

    - **Present Your Card**: Whenever you shop, present your loyalty card to accumulate points.

    - **Redeem Rewards**: Use accumulated points for discounts or special offers.

3. **Compare Prices Online Before Making Big Purchases**:

    - **Why?**: Online shopping provides convenience and access to a wide range of products.

    - **How?**:

        - **Research**: Use price comparison websites or apps to check prices across different online retailers.

- **Read Reviews**: Look for product reviews to ensure quality and reliability.

- **Consider Shipping Costs**: Factor in shipping fees when comparing prices.

4. **Buy Quality Over Quantity: Invest in Durable Items**:

   - **Why?**: Investing in well-made, durable items saves money in the long run.

   - **How?**:

     - **Assess Durability**: Consider the material, construction, and brand reputation.

     - **Avoid Fast Fashion**: Instead of buying multiple cheap items, invest in timeless pieces that last.

     - **Think Long-Term**: Quality shoes, bags, and kitchen appliances may cost more upfront but pay off over time.

Remember, being a savvy shopper doesn't mean sacrificing style or quality—it's about making informed choices that align with your budget and values. Happy shopping!

6 TRAVELLING

Traveling in the Philippines can be an incredible experience, and being well-prepared ensures you make the most of your trip. Let's dive into more details about these travel tips:

1. **Travel During Off-Peak Seasons**:

    - **Why?**: Off-peak seasons (outside major holidays and festivals) offer several advantages:

        - **Cheaper Flights**: Airlines often have lower fares during less busy times.
        - **Affordable Accommodations**: Hotels

and resorts may offer discounts.
- **Less Crowded**: Enjoy attractions without the crowds.

o **How?**: Research the specific off-peak periods for your chosen destinations. For example:

- **Boracay**: Avoid Holy Week (usually in April) and Christmas/New Year.
- **El Nido, Palawan**: Consider visiting between June and November.

2. **Use Public Transportation**:

o **Why?**: Public transportation is cost-effective and allows you to experience local life.

o **How?**:
- **Jeepneys**: Iconic Filipino jeeps—cheap and widely available.
- **Tricycles**: Motorcycle with a sidecar—common for short distances.

- **Buses and Vans**: Use them for intercity travel.
- **Ferries**: For island-hopping between the Philippines' 7,000+ islands.

3. **Book in Advance**:

    - **Why?**: Early bookings save money and ensure availability.

    - **How?**:
        - **Flights**: Book tickets well ahead, especially during peak seasons.
        - **Accommodations**: Reserve hotels or guesthouses in advance for better rates.
        - **Tours and Activities**: Secure spots for popular tours (e.g., island hopping, diving, hiking).

4. **Pack Light**:
5.
    - **Why?**: Excess baggage fees can add up, especially on domestic flights.

- **How?**:
  - **Choose Versatile Clothing**: Pack items that mix and match well.
  - **Limit Shoes**: Bring comfortable walking shoes and maybe one pair of sandals.
  - **Toiletries**: Opt for travel-sized items or buy locally.
  - **Laundry Options**: Many accommodations offer laundry services.

Remember, the Philippines is a diverse country with stunning beaches, lush mountains, and vibrant cities. Enjoy your trip, embrace the local culture, and savor every moment!

Let's dive deeper into entertainment tips in the Philippines, focusing on budget-friendly and enjoyable activities. Whether you're a local or a traveler, these ideas will help you have a great time without breaking the bank!

Entertainment Tips in the Philippines:

1. **Explore Free or Low-Cost Activities**:

    - **Parks**: Visit local parks for fresh air, exercise, and relaxation. Many parks have jogging paths, playgrounds, and picnic areas.
    - **Museums**: Discover the country's rich history and culture. The National Museum of the Philippines in Manila offers free admission to its various branches.
    - **Community Events**: Keep an eye out for festivals, art exhibits, and cultural performances. Check local listings for upcoming events.

2. **Host Potluck Gatherings**:

    - **Why?**: Sharing meals with friends and family is a wonderful way to bond.
    - **How?**:
        - **Invite Friends**: Host a potluck dinner at your place or a nearby park.
        - **Assign Dishes**: Ask each guest to bring a dish—appetizers, main course, or

dessert.
- **Enjoy the Variety**: Everyone gets to taste different homemade dishes without the burden of cooking everything yourself.

3. **Movie Nights at Home**:
4.
    - **Why?**: Create a cozy movie night without spending on cinema tickets.
    - **How?**:
        - **Choose a Theme**: Pick a genre (comedy, romance, sci-fi) or a series of movies.
        - **Make Popcorn**: Popcorn is a must! Add some flavor with herbs or cheese.
        - **Netflix or DVD**: Stream movies or watch your favorite DVDs.

Remember, entertainment doesn't have to be expensive—it's about enjoying moments with loved ones and exploring what the Philippines has to offer!

Spending quality time with family and friends doesn't have to break the bank. Let's explore these family-friendly and budget-conscious activities in the Philippines:

1. **Rotate Hosting Gatherings**:

    o **Why?**: Sharing the responsibility of hosting gatherings lightens the load and spreads the costs

    o **How?**:

      - **Potluck Dinners**: Each family takes turns hosting. Everyone brings a dish to share.

      - **Picnics or Barbecues**: Choose a park or beach, and everyone contributes food and drinks

      - **Game Nights**: Rotate game nights at different homes. Play board games, card games, or video games.

2. **Gift Creatively**:

    - **Why?**: Personalized gifts show thoughtfulness and save money compared to store-bought items.

    - **How?**:

        - **Homemade Treats**: Bake cookies, make jams, or create personalized recipe books.
        - **Handmade Crafts**: Knit scarves, paint mugs, or design custom T-shirts.
        - **Photo Albums**: Compile family photos into an album or scrapbook.

3. **Plan Group Outings**:

    - **Why?**: Group activities often come with discounts or group rates.
    - **How?**:
        - **Beach Trips**: Rent a van and split the cost for a beach getaway.
        - **Island-Hopping Tours**: Book as a group for better rates.

- **Theme Parks or Water Parks**: Many offer group discounts.

Remember, it's the shared experiences and meaningful connections that matter most. Whether it's a potluck dinner, a homemade gift, or a day at the beach, cherish these moments with your loved ones!

7 HEALTH MATTERS

Taking care of your health is essential, and I'm here to provide more details on maintaining a healthy lifestyle in the Philippines. Let's dive into these health tips:

1. **Eat a Healthy Diet**:

    - **Why?**: A balanced diet supports overall health and reduces the risk of noncommunicable diseases (NCDs) like diabetes, heart disease, and cancer.

- **How?**:

    - **Include Fruits and Vegetables**: Aim for at least five portions (400g) daily. Vary your choices and eat them in season.
    - **Limit Salt and Sugar**: Reduce salt intake to 5g per day (about one teaspoon). Limit sugary snacks and beverages.

2. **Reduce Intake of Harmful Fats**:

    - **Why?**: Unhealthy fats contribute to weight gain and NCDs.

    - **How?**:

        - **Choose Unsaturated Fats**: Found in fish, avocado, nuts, and oils like sunflower, soybean, canola, and olive.
        - **Limit Saturated and Trans Fats**: Found in fatty meat, butter, palm oil, and pre-packaged snacks.

3. **Avoid Harmful Use of Alcohol**:

    o **Why?**: Alcohol can lead to health problems, including liver cirrhosis, cancers, and mental disorders.
    o **How?**: There is no safe level for drinking alcohol. Consider alternatives to alcohol for socializing.

4. **Exercise Outdoors**:

    o **Why?**: Outdoor exercise is free and beneficial for physical and mental health.
    o **How?**: Walk, jog, cycle, or do yoga in parks or natural surroundings

5. **Cook Nutritious Meals**:

    o **Why?**: Homemade meals are healthier and prevent medical expenses.

    o **How?**:
      - **Plan Balanced Meals**: Include whole grains, lean proteins, fruits, and vegetables.

- **Limit Processed Foods**: Cook from scratch to control ingredients.

6. **Practice Preventive Care**:

    - **Why?**: Regular check-ups detect health issues early, preventing costly treatments later.
    - **How?**: Schedule routine visits to your doctor, dentist, and other specialists.

Remember, small lifestyle changes add up over time, leading to better health and financial well-being!

8 WORK RELATED ISSUES

Let's delve into more details about work-related tips, including salary negotiation and company benefits in the Philippines. Whether you're starting a new job or looking to enhance your existing employment situation, these insights can be valuable.

Salary Negotiation: Know Your Worth

1. **Research and Prepare**:

    o Understand industry standards and salary ranges for your role.
    o Consider your experience, skills, and

- market demand.
- Be ready to justify your desired salary with specific achievements and contributions.

2. **Timing Matters**:

    - Negotiate during the job offer stage.
    - Highlight your value and express enthusiasm for the role.

3. **Be Assertive but Polite**:

    - State your desired salary confidently.
    - Use positive language and avoid being confrontational.

4. **Consider Total Compensation**:

    - Look beyond base salary: consider bonuses, benefits, and perks.
    - Negotiate health insurance, retirement plans, and other non-monetary benefits.

Company Benefits in the Philippines
1. **Mandatory Benefits**:

    - **Social Security System (SSS)**: Provides retirement, disability, and health benefits.

    - **PhilHealth**: Mandatory health insurance for employees.

    - **Pag-IBIG Fund**: Housing and provident fund contributions.

    - **13th-Month Pay**: Equivalent to one month's salary, typically given in December.

2. **Supplemental Benefits**:

    - **Health Insurance**: Some companies offer comprehensive health coverage.

    - **Retirement Plans**: Consider employer-sponsored retirement funds.

- **Leave Entitlements**: Vacation, sick leave, and maternity/paternity leave.

Remember, understanding both your worth and the available benefits ensures a balanced and rewarding work experience!

9 ADDITIONAL INFORMATION

Improving your negotiation skills is valuable in both personal and professional contexts. Whether you're aiming for better deals, stronger relationships, or career advancement, here are some strategies to enhance your negotiation prowess:

Track Your Negotiations:

Habitually track your negotiations. Document everyday interactions—whether it's resolving conflicts with friends or making small requests.
Use a journal or digital notes to record negotiation details, outcomes, and lessons learned.
Regularly review your negotiation experiences to identify patterns and areas for improvement.

Reflect on Past Negotiations:

After tracking your negotiations, take time to reflect on them.
Consider questions like:
What worked well in certain situations?
When did you feel confident or uncertain?
Were there missed opportunities to create value?
Self-reflection helps you understand your strengths, preferences, and negotiation best practices.

Learn How to Create Value:

Negotiation isn't just about dividing a fixed pie; it's about expanding the pie.
Understand the concept of the "zone of possible agreement" (ZOPA). Identify areas where both parties can benefit.
Focus on mutual gains rather than zero-sum thinking.
Develop Emotional Intelligence Skills:
Emotional intelligence (EQ) plays a crucial role in negotiations.
Practice active listening, empathy, and understanding your own emotions.
Recognize emotions in others and adapt your approach accordingly.

Build Confidence:

Confidence positively impacts negotiation outcomes.
Prepare thoroughly, know your facts, and practice your pitch.
Remember that negotiation is a skill that improves with practice.

Pursue Learning Opportunities:

Take negotiation courses or workshops.
Read books, listen to podcasts, and follow negotiation experts.

Learn from real-world examples and case studies.
Remember, negotiation is an art, and continuous learning and practice will make you a more effective and confident negotiator!

Emotional intelligence (EI) plays a significant role in negotiation, impacting how effectively we navigate conflicts, build rapport, and achieve win-win outcomes. Let's explore this further:

Understanding Emotional Intelligence (EI):

EI refers to the ability to recognize, understand, and manage our own emotions and those of others.

It involves self-awareness, self-regulation, empathy, and social skills.

Why EI Matters in Negotiation:

Empathy: EI enables negotiators to empathize with the other party's perspective, demonstrating genuine interest in understanding their needs and concerns.

Active Listening: EI helps negotiators actively listen, acknowledge emotions, and validate viewpoints. This fosters trust and creates a conducive environment for constructive dialogue.

Emotion Regulation: EI allows negotiators to manage their own emotions during tense moments. Remaining calm and composed enhances decision-making.

EI Strategies for Effective Negotiation:

Recognize Emotional Cues: Pay attention to verbal and nonverbal cues from your counterpart. Understand their emotional state.

Adapt Communication Style: Tailor your approach based on the other party's emotions. Be flexible and responsive.

Build Trust: EI helps you build rapport and trust. Trust is essential for successful negotiations.

Manage Conflict: EI allows you to address conflicts constructively. Avoid escalating emotions.

Case Example:

Imagine negotiating a salary increase with your employer. High EI would involve:
Understanding your own feelings (e.g., nervousness, excitement).
Recognizing your employer's emotions (e.g., concern about budget constraints).
Using empathy to find common ground (e.g., emphasizing your value to the company).
Maintaining a positive tone and seeking a mutually beneficial outcome.
Remember, EI is a skill that can be developed over time. Practice self-awareness, active listening, and empathy—it will enhance your negotiation abilities!

Emotional intelligence is a powerful tool in negotiation, allowing us to connect, understand, and collaborate effectively

Active listening is a powerful communication skill that goes beyond merely hearing what someone says.

It involves being fully present, engaged, and empathetic during conversations. When you actively listen, you not only understand the content of the message but also pick up on emotions, nonverbal cues, and underlying meanings.

Let's explore some active listening techniques:

Restate what the speaker said in your own words. This shows that you're paying attention and helps clarify any misunderstandings.

Example: "So, if I understand correctly, you're concerned about the upcoming project deadline?"

Nod and Smile:
Nonverbal cues matter. Nodding and smiling encourage the speaker and signal your engagement.
Example: Nodding while saying, "I see what you mean."

Ask Open-Ended Questions:
Encourage deeper conversation by asking questions that can't be answered with a simple "yes" or "no."
Example: "What led you to that conclusion?"

Ask Specific Probing Questions:
Dig deeper into specific aspects of the topic.
Example: "Could you elaborate on how that situation made you feel?"

Use Short Verbal Affirmations:
Show your interest and understanding with brief statements like "I see," "Got it," or "Interesting."

Display Empathy:
Put yourself in the speaker's shoes. Acknowledge their emotions.
Example: "It sounds like you're feeling frustrated about the changes."
Share Similar Experiences:
Relate to the speaker by sharing relevant personal experiences.
Example: "I remember when I faced a similar challenge at work."
Recall Previously Shared Information:
Refer back to what the speaker mentioned earlier. It shows you've been actively listening.
Example: "Earlier, you mentioned that teamwork was crucial for this project."
Avoid Distracting Movements:
Maintain eye contact and avoid fidgeting or checking your phone.

Remember, active listening builds trust, strengthens relationships, and enhances communication. Practice these techniques, and you'll become a more effective and empathetic listener!

Visit Arthurcrandon.co.uk for More Titles

Retirement to the Philippines
K1 Fiance visa to the U.S. – Fast Track
Secrets to buying Condos in the Philippines
Buying Land in the Philippines
Annulment in the Philippines
Breaking free from a bad marriage
Get a visit visa to America First time
Marriage in the Philippines
Get a visit visa to the United Kingdom
Ghosts, Spectres, and folklore in the Philippines
Retiring to Spain – a Comprehensive Guide
Spousal Visa to America
Spousal visa to the United Kingdom
Working in the UK.
Working in the US.

ABOUT THE AUTHOR

Arthur Crandon is a retired lawyer and a prolific writer. He is British and grew up in a rural community in Somerset. He has lived in England, Wales, Hong Kong and the Philippines and now spends most of his time in the Philippines with his Visayan wife and their son.

He loves to hear from anyone who has anything to do with the Philippines – you can email him anytime on:

ac@arthurcrandon.co.uk

www.ingramcontent.com/pod-product-compliance
Lightning Source LLC
Chambersburg PA
CBHW070413230526
45471CB00006B/2777